WANDA DARKSTAR

By Jane A C West

Illustrated by
Anthony Williams

Titles in the Zipwire series:

Who Are You?	David Orme
3Dee	Danny Pearson
Doom Clone	Melanie Joyce
Too Risky!	Alison Hawes
Wanda Darkstar	Jane A C West
Galactic Games	Roger Hurn
Robot Eyes	Jillian Powell
Charlie's Tin	Lynda Gore
Run For Your Life	Jonny Zucker
Changing Rooms	Melanie Joyce

Badger Publishing Limited
Oldmedow Road, Hardwick Industrial Estate,
King's Lynn PE30 4JJ
Telephone: 01553 769209
www.badgerlearning.co.uk

4 6 8 10 9 7 5 3

Wanda Darkstar ISBN 978-1-78837-604-4

Text © Jane A C West 2011
Complete work © Badger Publishing Limited 2021

All rights reserved. No part of this publication may be reproduced, stored in any form or by any means mechanical, electronic, recording or otherwise without the prior permission of the publisher.

The right of Jane A C West to be identified as author of this Work has been asserted by her in accordance with the Copyright, Designs and Patents Act 1988.

Badger Publishing would like to thank Jonny Zucker for his help in putting this series together.

Commissioning Editor: Sarah Rudd
Editor: Claire Morgan
Typesetting: Adam Wilmott
Illustration: Anthony Williams
Page 32 illustration: Juliet Breese
Cover design: Shaun Page
Font: OpenDyslexic

WANDA DARKSTAR

Contents

Chapter 1	5
Chapter 2	10
Chapter 3	13
Chapter 4	17
Chapter 5	23
Questions	30

Chapter 1

This might shock you.

Earth isn't as alone as most humans think.

Lots of aliens live here.

I should know.

I'm one of them.

My name is Wanda Darkstar.

My job is to make sure aliens live happily here on Earth.

The number one rule is to NEVER tell the humans that aliens exist.

I teach the aliens how to act like humans.

I tell them things like:

Watch Football.

Hide your tentacles.

Don't eat cat litter!

Rex Squid didn't see why he should pretend to be a human.

"Because it's the law!" I told him.

"When you got your passport for Earth, you agreed to keep your real self hidden," I said.

I thought that was the end of it.

I was wrong.

Chapter 2

I scanned the area for problems.

It was going to be a bad day.

"Rex Squid has left isolation!" I told the team.

Aliens have to isolate until they are ready to mix with humans.

But Rex was on his way to the bus station.

I had to get there quickly, but my starship was being fixed.

I had no choice.

I had to take the scooter.

Chapter 3

I caught up with Rex.

He wasn't hiding his true alien form!

"What is that?" a scared woman cried.

"That's my uncle," I said. "Brilliant costume, isn't it?"

"Oh... yes," she said faintly.

Then she asked, "How does he do the slime trail?"

I pretended not to hear her.

Rex had his tentacles on show.

He was handing out leaflets for his new book, My Life on Earth.

I had to move quickly.

Luckily, most people don't read leaflets they are given in the street.

Chapter 4

Rex had moved on to the bus station.

There was a big crowd.

Rex wasn't going to make it easy for me.

Rex was checking out the bus timetable.

He was looking at buses to London.

Not on my watch!

Suddenly, Rex turned around and came straight towards me.

"What do you want, Darkstar?" he asked.

"You know I can't let you do this, Rex," I replied. "You've got to come with me."

"No way!" he shouted. "I am sick of acting like a human. I want everyone on Earth to see the real me."

"That won't happen, Rex. Don't make me zap you," I warned.

If I zap an alien, they have to spend the rest of their life frozen in human form.

"You won't zap me!" cried Rex.

"Only if I have to," I told him.

"You wouldn't dare zap me in front of the humans!" Rex jeered.

He was right.

And now a man was walking up to us.

Chapter 5

"I'd like to talk to you about your flyer..." the man said.

"It's a cool costume, isn't it?" I said quickly.

"It's no costume!" shouted Rex.

I had to take control of
the situation.

"Uncle Rex! I feel sick!" I cried.

I grabbed hold of Rex's arm.

I managed to drag Rex away.

It's easier to drag someone with tentacles than someone with feet!

"One day the humans will have to know the truth. Why not today?" asked Rex.

"They aren't ready," I replied.

"We could rule this planet," said Rex.

He had gone too far.

He knew it.

"Don't zap me!" he cried.

But I had no choice.

"Sorry, Rex," I said. "I have to keep the humans safe."

I zapped him.

But something went wrong.

The zap ray was supposed to freeze Rex in human form, but he was shrinking.

Rex was now a human child!

He was furious.

I tried not to smile.

I got back on my scooter.

I needed to tell the galactic police about Rex.

They would know what to do with him.

Another day in the life of Wanda Darkstar!

Questions

Why does Wanda take her scooter instead of her starship? *(page 11)*

What is Rex's book called? *(page 15)*

What happens if an alien gets zapped? *(page 21)*

What happens to Rex? *(page 28)*

zipwire

Looking for your next read?

Have a look at all the great books in the Zipwire series

badgerlearning.co.uk   @badgerlearning